Traces of Heaven

A Spiritual Guide to Life After Life

Nancine Meyer, CSC/CSSP
Certified Spiritual Counselor
and Angel Clairvoyant

Copyright © 2019 by Nancine Meyer

All book rights reserved. This or any portion holder, except by a reviewer, who may quote thereof may not be reproduced or used in any form or by any electronic or mechanical means including information storage and retrieval systems without permission from the copyright in brief passages a review.

Library of Congress Control Number: 2019913142

ISBN: 978-1-950943-00-5

First Printing: October 2019

Cover Design: Deb Manning Design
                     Ft. Myers Beach, FL 33931

Publisher: 102nd Place, LLC
                     Cave Creek, AZ 85331

What Others are Saying

Traces of Heaven is an absolute joy to read. As a long-time Spiritualist and Medium, I found this book to be refreshing and informative. Often, there is a tendency to over-complicate spirituality. Nancine's easygoing approach to discovering your own spiritual gifts is a delight. In these pages, you will find answers to the age-old questions of what happens when we die, where do we go, and is communication with those who have passed on possible? With gentle humor and easy to understand instruction, this book will encourage newcomers and experienced seekers of the truth alike to explore the realms of communication with angels, spirit guides, and your loved ones, or as Nancine refers to them, the Sweet Ones. *Traces of Heaven* is a must-read for anyone wishing to broaden their spiritual horizons!

Sheila Leedy
Spiritualist Medium, Speaker and Teacher

I like to think of Nancine Meyer as a unique, entertaining "energy mechanic." *Traces of Heaven* is an excellent and refreshing example of her art. With encouragement, this book reminds us of our true spiritual origin even while we explore a material world. It then takes the reader further along life's journey to see just exactly why we came here and how eternal and joyful life after life really is. You will learn communication tools to reach loved ones no longer in your physical presence, and you will get a glance at what you too may expect after death by reading about the 5 Stages of Afterlife. Without a doubt, Nancine is an extraordinary spiritual teacher who writes with heavenly angel guidance. This is a book you will enjoy not just once but refer to again and again. It is my privilege to invite you to read *Traces of Heaven.*

Mary Lou Chapman
Angel Clairvoyant/Counselor, Psychometrist, Ordained Minister
https://www.TrustYourAngels.com

Dedicated to the many Angels surrounding us

With special gratitude to my Guardian Angels,

Michael Benjamin, Dawn, and Surely

Foreword

In my many years as an intuitive business coach, I have helped my clients identify their special talents and align them with the life they desire to create. For example, some people may be gifted with singing or dancing or any of the Arts. Others are blessed with natural abilities in design, formation, communication, or scientific fields. Of course, there are many combinations across the talent spectrum. If you are reading this book, you know that in the same fashion of blessings, there are those people whose gifts are of a spiritual nature. These individuals are set apart with a grace to not only understand, but also to see into other dimensions where God, angels, spirit guides, and all celestial beings reside. Nancine Meyer is one of those persons.

Since age five, Nancine has enjoyed an extrasensory sight and dialogue with celestial angels. Over the years, Nancine's natural gift invited her curiosity and subsequent communication with other spiritual beings, including acting as an intermediary for those who have died. Whether she is personally coaching, speaking, or writing, Nancine enjoys infusing her understood spirituality into her material work. It is not surprising that she has become one of the most accurate, loving, and highly respected sixth sensory teachers and psychic guides in our present day. As an author, she has previously delighted us with her spiritual knowledge and personal stories in the book, *The Lighter Side of Prayer.*

Now, in the pages to follow, Nancine brings to us her newest work, *Traces of Heaven.* In her uniquely playful yet compassionate style, she shares with us a summary of all that angels have revealed to her about the journey individuals take – from spiritual beginning to material birth, to death, and the transition back to our true Home. For the first time, you will read the angels' channeled narrative of the *Five Stages of Afterlife*, in which, importantly, many of the questions recurring when a loved one dies will be answered.

Traces of Heaven is filled with stories, tools, and insights to ease your fears and bring peace to your heart. You'll want to return to it often as a guide to increasing your connection with those you love who are now on the mystical Other Side. This is a book which indeed brings a treasure trove of spiritual awakening right to you wherever you may be.

Tina Ferguson, Author
The Road's End & Infinite Forgiveness: How to Easily Forgive Yourself and Others

Contents

Foreword i

Introduction... 1

Part One Comparing Life and Life After 7

    The Unified Vibrational Field 9

    Defining Spiritual Beings 13

        Human Beings 13

        Spirit Guides 15

        Ascended Masters 16

        Angels and the Angel Hierarchy 18

        The Deceased 23

Part Two The Spiritual Being's Journey 27

    The New World 29

    Moving Day 35

    The Healing Pod 39

    The 5 Stages of Afterlife 43

        Surprise 45

        Concern 47

        Attunement 48

        Acceptance 50

        Bliss 51

Part Three Conversations with Heaven 53

    The Wish to Connect 55

Sending and Receiving 59
Learning Symbolism 75
Fine-Tuning Our Good Senses 81

Part Four The Present Moment 85
The Fading Memory 87
"You Are Here" 91
From "Here" On 95

Part Five Until We Meet Again 99
Human Resilience 101
Skin Hunger 105
Fear of Abandonment 107
Life After Life 113

About the Author 119

Gratitudes 121

Introduction

As we move along our present life's journey, we emotionally connect with others whose lives, by design, cross with ours. The most intimate of these relationships are those with family and friends whom we deeply cherish. Within any of the personal conversations with those closest to us, we may have talked at one time or another about human mortality and a spiritual world unknown. We speculate about this otherworldly place (or places) and imagine its whereabouts in relation to ours, but we first begin to really question whether or not it exists when someone very close to us dies.

Do you wonder about the well-being of those who have died? Are you curious about their possible spiritual visits to your side? The pages and stories following will ease your concerns, answer many of your questions, and validate your paranormal experiences. In addition, if you wonder about what may happen to you after your last breath in the physical world, the Five Stages of Afterlife, shared for the first time in this book, may reduce the fear projected upon the dying process.

As you are aware, we are physically blessed with Five Great Senses: Sight, Hearing, Smell, Touch, and Taste. As spiritual beings – which we primarily are – it is important to realize that we have six senses, not merely five. The Sixth Sense is our natural intuitiveness or extrasensory perception, and might more properly be referred to as the First Sense because of its accurate guidance for the best possible way of life.

Sadly, this extraordinary insight is too often not accessed because of our effortless reliance upon the five senses to move about within our solid, physical world. Fortunately, our Sixth Sense is always at hand and will never expire.

Some professional training is one good choice for stimulating its regular involvement in all your situations. Quality psychic training of any kind will focus on discerning "true" guidance which is spiritual from "false" guidance which is mental or ego, learning your communication strength or strengths (see, hear, feel, know), and learning signs for a mutually understood spiritual language. Much of the remaining development involves practice, practice, practice, and increasing trust in the process.

Along my own life journey, ever since the age of five, I have always enjoyed the company of angels: seeing, hearing, feeling, and knowing them at my side and around others. From that young age, it was the angels surrounding me who guided me to my teachers and sixth sensory development. It was the angels at my side who moved me on from my connection with them for my sole benefit to teaching and connecting others with their angels, as well as becoming a guide or conduit of messaging with deceased loved ones now on the Other Side. This began my work as a spiritual coach and angel medium.

I ask you to trust that all of my writing herein has been attended to and inspired by the angels around me, including those who are, by design, authors. The angels of whom I speak are the pure energy beings who have never taken on a physical body; they have instead remained at the innermost, highest energy placement within the Unified Vibrational Field. They are closest to Source (God). Because of this divine placement, their guidance is 100% pure. These angels connect with us whenever we ask, in whatever manner is loving, supportive, and gentle. They whisper, not yell. They "nudge," not command. They guide, not decide. There is no task too great or too small for which they will not gently and readily assist us. These amazing Light Beings are always available to each and all of us, and I encourage you to develop a relationship with them.

Throughout this book, I will often refer to deceased loved ones as the "Sweet Ones." I began using this term for these spirits after unique yet similar encounters with them. I found each one who I connect with reveals a number of distinct personality traits developed while on the earth. Certainly, this helps share evidentiary messaging. Yet, without exception, they each speak with the same sweet and loving voice (hello) to me; thus, I call them collectively the *Sweet Ones.*

As you begin to read, keep in mind, we are without exception spiritual beings, choosing a humanly designed experience. It is not the other way around. We are by our nature always connected to God, angels, spiritual guides, and our deceased loved ones who returned Home. *Traces of Heaven* will give you answers to your quest for inter-world communication.

Finally, and most importantly, this is a guide to awaken your spiritual memory so you may advance your joy along your present travel on earth. Each of us came here for a period of time with a divine purpose created with our Source of Love. The original idea was to animate such Love in a basic world. Instead, the beauty and wealth of the solid earth encouraged material needs and contentment great enough to cause spiritual amnesia.

Fortunately, we are blessed with an internal cue to refresh our primary goal; that is, an uninterrupted feeling of Bliss. Therefore, you can trust that whenever you are not feeling completely joyful in any present moment, something is "off." It is an intrinsic signal that your True Spirit is serving worldly distractions, rather than the other way around. Another way to say this is that we have a learned tendency to allow our mental being to reverse the order of our true Life-Force. So, I believe it's time we set this right for our True Spirits.

Traces of Heaven will begin this healing. It was written over time with your angels' love and direction. It is my greatest wish for you that after reading these simple stories and instructions, you will comfortably remember your Truth, reclaim your connection with all spiritual beings, and welcome an active part in your own amazing journey back Home. I wish you epiphanies, synchronicities, and angels all around you to light your way. May this or something greater happen for you and your highest good, which is the highest good of All!

All my love & blessings,

Nancine

PART ONE

Comparing Life and Life-After

The Unified Vibrational Field

Since one purpose of this book is to ease the mystery attached to the relationship of our physical world and the spirit world, a little understanding of the Unified Vibrational Field is a good place to begin.

When you look at the small-scale image [Fig.1], you will notice there are many levels of energy rings which make up the wholly connected spiral referred to as the Unified Vibrational Field. Looking at it more closely, you will see there is no disconnect between any of the rings nor any from the Center (Source). This Center is fixed and radiates as the highest field of vibration, light, and creation. From the Center, in either direction across the spiral, there are varying intensities of energy and light emanating and interacting. Please understand, this Fig. 1 image is but a small-scale representation, and the actual spiral of All Energy is, of course, vast in degree by comparison. The illustration is simply to help you recall two important factors for understanding and comparison of the life-we-know to the lives-after.

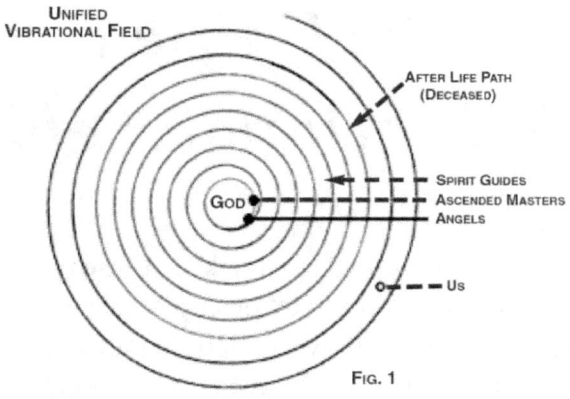

Fig. 1

First, there is no disconnect between any or all of us within the energy spiral regardless of our present form. All are an equal part of its Whole. Therefore, we most certainly can and do communicate. However, the second notable fact is the farther out from Center any individual is in its present form, the slower or denser the transmission of their concentrated energy. You can see, because of our present physicality, we humans, (Us) are resting at the outermost rim and therefore live with the greatest energy density compared to our spiritual partners. This heaviness of our present form is why we cannot readily "see" our non-bodily partners with our physical eyes, and thus, we perceive separation.

The separation we recognize between us, the physically embodied, and those disembodied beings (spiritual or deceased) is what has popularly become labeled "the veil;" a division made by "heaven and earth." In reality, there is no uncoupling between us and any other life forces who are ethereal-shaped energy beings. There is undeniably a dialogue barrier to overcome between the two worlds of dissimilar *form*. The primary difficulty is our very contrasting speeds of transmitting ideas. Because of such variance, messaging between worlds demands a mutually understood translation. We can accomplish this shared narrative by the use of our extrasensory ability. While we each have extrasensory skill, most of us limit our exercise of such talent to gut feelings and impressions within our physical world. An extension of our natural psychic abilities is necessary when messaging through the "veil."

One choice may be a medium inasmuch as he/she has an innate sensitivity for exchanging messages with the rapid vibrations of those in the spirit world: angels, spirit guides, or Sweet Ones. However, many everyday people are able to study and train their sixth sensory selves to speak and receive messages clearly between worlds.

Just as it is with any bilingual learning, sixth sensory messaging requires interest, willingness, and patience. The first course of self-development requires learning both universal and individualized signs and symbols to provide quick, mostly accurate deciphering. Consistency of exchange and a balance between sending and receiving are critical to advance success.

Let's take a closer look at each type of spiritual group connected to each other by means of the Unified Vibrational Field.

Defining Spiritual Beings

Human Beings

As difficult as it may be to grasp, humans are primarily spiritual beings who are living in a physical environment. We are each here on earth by choice and with a self-created design to magnify the 100% pure love and joy of a heavenly Origin wherein all are within One. We intended to recreate our essential knowledge of Source in a tangible dimension, for a period of time. We did not anticipate with our spirits' physical transformation all the created beauty of mind and matter would cause our life-force to drift from its holy intention. This is, however, what happens. Because the immortal being is now contained within a material body, celestial power is doused in denser energy. This reduces the Spirit to maneuvering through physical faculties. In our present form as human beings, we respond to everything experienced as a wholly separate, solid environment. Unfortunately, this limited mental response also influences human perception of anything contrary; including the spirit world of which we are part.

Human beings are meant to enjoy all material creations of the earth and universe because all are created to serve our story in this world. What is important is that we realize we are here for the earth to contribute to our divine purpose and not distract us from it. At a very subtle level of being, we know we have our sense of order reversed and seek to correct it. What interrupts this underlying wisdom is the thickness of our present energy overbearing the light, airy whispers of our Higher Self. We do, however, sense its presence when we hear ourselves utter, "there must be something more" or "it wasn't supposed to be this way." Daydreaming in this direction is one signal we have some remembering to do.

The easiest way to trigger the spiritual memory of who we are and what we came here to do is to ask our True (innermost) Spirit, "Spirit, what is my divine purpose?" As with all questions, the more you ask, the more you will learn. It is a good practice to pause other activity while you are asking, and allow time to receive any new sense of imagining. There will be more examples of working with your True Spirit in the pages to follow.

Spirit Guides

This group of spiritual beings are those who, similar to us, lived on a material plane at one time. They capably understand the joys and tribulations of a physical life experience and continue to hold the imprint of the knowledge and proficiency acquired in that lifetime. Some may have been leaders or experts in a profession or career; others were celebrities in the arts and sciences. Many others served in simple roles while on earth in which they became highly respected: a painter, a writer, a handy person. The common factor is that *all* spirit guides who were highly proficient in their material lives retain such wisdom and skill in the spirit world, and their particular talent continues to be theirs to share from the Other Side.

You may call upon any of the spirit guides according to your specific need for support. Other times they may be drawn to your work because it is something which they love and have mastered. You may not see these spiritual leaders, but you will notice greater ease in the project or challenge before you. Some of these guides may be deceased family members or friends; others, simply ascended persons with a particular skill. By celestial groups, they are defined as teachers, helpers, runners, healers and joy-givers. Interestingly, because spirit guides were once human, and due to the likelihood of our own Spirits having had "past lives," sometimes when a guide's energy is near, we feel a familiarity. We call this déjà vu.

The value in raising awareness to spirit guides is most certainly the supernatural mentoring in ready supply for our human creations and effort. Spirit guides are ready and eager to share their aptitude anytime you *invite* them. Notably, the key word is "invite." All spirit guides only interject their help because they are interested in sharing the wisdom they own. Without our request or agreement, they do not interfere with our earthly life stories. It may be easiest to think of spirit guides as a search engine on the Other Side. At this very moment, many more Sweet Ones are training to become spirit guides. As you excel in your roles on earth, this may well be you one day.

Ascended Masters

The term "Ascended Masters" refers to any of those spiritual beings who manifested, as did we, within a physical body for a period of time. The exception to the commonality of experience is that each one participated as a universal healer, teacher, or mystic during their presence here. Notably, throughout their lifetime in a physical body, they retained super-consciousness. This is saying that throughout their physical lifetime, they were aware they were God-connected, spiritual beings creating in a material expression. They acquired no emotional attachment to their physical experience; thus, their God-energy remained pure. Because of their preserved state of enlightenment while walking on earth, their light-speed was immediately restored to its original maximum after death. This is why you will find this group's placement close to Center on the Universal Vibrational Field. Comparatively, human beings experience a gradual flow back into their fullness of divine energy after death.

We have witnessed or studied accounts of many Ascended Masters who were once on earth. Among such prominent persons were Jesus, Moses, Buddha, Mary of Nazareth, and more. Some others ascended from their famous roles in history, science, and the arts. Still others include those we define as saints, gods and goddesses, and bodhisattvas once among us.

Now returned to spirit, the intelligence of all Ascended Masters is multicultural and not sectarian; meaning no one Master is limited to the role they played on earth. This then assures us their guidance and influence are available to each of us without regard to our present religious, cultural, or other affiliation. In addition, Ascended Masters are of a universal energy that can be in many places at the same time; thus, you cannot deprive someone else of their assistance while you are asking for it for yourself. Think of these divine beings as a *Council of Eternal Wisdom*. They are ready to enlighten your ability to heal, evolve, and accomplish your divine purpose here. All you have to do is ask and attune yourself to hearing their message.

Angels and the Angel Hierarchy

Looking again at the energy spiral [Fig. 1], you will notice the position of angels is a solid mark closest to Center (God). This is because angels are uniquely different from all other spiritual beings including ourselves and deceased loved ones. Our angel friends are *fixed in proximity* to Source for all eternity and, with rare exception, have never assumed a human body or lived a physical life. This means angels are incredibly powerful spiritual beings because their energy has never been flawed by physical rebirth. It is valuable to understand that, because angels remain wholly and perpetually at Home (Center) as pure spiritual beings, their guidance is a mirror-vibration of God's Love, Light, and Intelligence. They are loving spirits and do not judge humanness because they only see the goodness and power of your True Spirit of God.

There are several kinds of glorious rhythms

emanating from angels. There are those who echo the 100% Love of God, our Center. These angels are collectively called the cherubim, seraphim, and thrones. You hear them in every harp, drum, trumpet, and holy song. Those angels who reflect God's thoughts of balance and truth are groups called dominions, virtues, powers, and principalities. They watch over the order of the universe and galaxies, so you may feel their energy when you are silently stargazing. A final angel group is made up of those angels who offer their celestial assistance to earth and physical beings. These spirits include archangels, guardian angels, elemental or nature angels, and what I call "situation angels." Because it is easiest for human beings to communicate with the group of angels assigned to earth, following is a greater understanding of those within it.

- **Archangels** are comparable to what we might term management. They coordinate earthly angels' specialties according to specific human needs. For example, Archangel Michael assigns angel protection and delivery of courage. Archangel Gabriel oversees communication accuracy of all kinds. Raphael supervises effective healing and guiding of healers. Uriel directs the advancement of new ideas and the easing of transitions. Archangel Chamuel commands those angels who relieve human anxiety and sense of loss. There are many more archangels inasmuch as there are many human conditions and needs to which God's love attends. Books listing archangel names along with "who does what" are available for your further curiosity. Even without specific names, you may call for an archangel's help according to the challenge you are facing; e.g., archangel of healing, archangel of clarity, archangel of protection.

- **Elementals** or nature angels are those who guard, nourish, and balance all characteristics of Earth and all the living things upon it. These diminutive faeries and sprites watch over our flora and fauna and command respect for all of earth's landscape. They are the glisten upon the water's crest and the flicker within a flame. You feel their energy when you cuddle your pet, lean toward a plant, smell a flower, or sit beneath a tree. You might even hear a giggle or a whisper of "grow, grow" when you are nearby their world. Just remember, anytime you are within or near any part of nature, these precious light beings are showering you with gentleness and joy. Is it any wonder that health experts encourage us to go outside more often?

- **Situation Angels** are similar to nature angels in size, but with a focus on ordinary human situations as they arise. There is no situation or need you find yourself within that is too great or too small for their solution or help. You simply call upon them by the named circumstance for which you would like some assistance; for example, parking angels, shopping angels, romance angels, money angels, career angels, travel angels, and so on. The groups are as endless as the conditions you may imagine, and you'll be amazed by the solutions you receive. I encourage you to try any of the above.

- **Guardian Angels** are your personal, accessible delight. Just like the rest of the angel hierarchy, they have no "space restriction." However, these angels have *chosen* to remain in a fixed energy space with a familiar, once-spiritual being who decided to make a physical transition. They remain constant at the individual's side from the point of heavenly departure, throughout the person's life on earth, and until the individual returns to spiritual form. We each walk about with at least two such guardian angels in our present energy field. If you consider the fact we chose to "come to" earth and manifest Love, it is not so difficult to understand that your guardian angels are your best friends whom you knew at Home in the cosmos. They are fully aware of your personal mission on earth and forever tag along as your exclusive assistants. Their gifts to you are visible to my sensory eyes when I read for you. Additionally, since guardian angels stick with their person not only on earth but thereafter, they are of divine value in assisting all of us with inter-world, spiritual communication.

All of the above-named types and many more unmentioned, fill out the Angel Hierarchy. Remember again that because angel energy has never been altered or hindered by a physical transition, it only emits 100% of God's Love, Light, and Intelligence. Their guidance is trustworthy, and they do not judge human choices or mistakes. They see, as does Source, only the goodness and power of your true Spirit. Speak to these angels by name, occupation, or situation. All you have to do is "ask" and "listen." Coincidentally, the first letter of their name is "A" and the last is "L." What is more, I once teased the angels, "what does the N.G.E. in the middle of your name mean?" They were quick to respond: "**N**o **G**reat **E**ffort."

Finally, here's a look at the remaining group of spiritual beings shown on the Unified Vibrational Field.

The Deceased

The label "deceased" is one which is assigned to all spiritual beings who have lived in the physical life dimension and have since shed the physical body. This shedding or end of mortality is eventual for each of us who at one time elected physical consciousness and material world experiences. After the material body is dead, the spiritual being formerly within it is restored to its original ethereal expression. Each spiritual being then travels a return path in the universal energy world toward God-self (Center).

The pace of each refreshed spirit's journey toward the infinite Center varies for each new arrival. This is partly explained by the mixture of emotional needs and personality traits which remained in the deceased's aura upon the spirit's release. Think of these lingering needs and traits as "souvenirs," which were collected on earth within the presence of material people, places, and things. Similar to any understanding of a souvenir, how long these reminders are held onto is the owner's choice. The angels do point out, the longer our returned spirit is reminded of its past material life with souvenirs, the slower the transformation to highest, lightest, and eternal form. Nonetheless, while each deceased person's freed spirit will differ in restoration, there is no judgment or comparison in our heavens. All will eventually reach the crowning point.

I know you are eager to know more about communicating in particular with this last spiritual group, and more instructions will follow later on. In general, when you communicate with deceased loved ones, take into account that any exchange with them is affected by where their present place in divine restoration may be. I mention this because we tend to immediately canonize loved ones who have died, and frequently pray for their advice for our decisions here on earth. When you do, understand your loved one's advice is likely not *divine* guidance as is true of angels, Ascended Masters, and spirit guides. Depending on the number of years of return, the Sweet Ones' input is more likely colored with remnants of their earthly personality. This means the advice you feel a loved one offered (e.g., a response to "should I buy this house?") is no more spiritually advanced than the advice they gave when here in your presence. So, to be frank, you may "take it or leave it" without any guilt or regret.

Don't let this deter your connecting with the Sweet Ones; just curb any quick decisions resulting from their perceived guidance. In all things important to your physical, mental, and emotional well-being, it is better to receive direction from the angels and stick with simple socializing for the newly deceased. One day, with a longer amount of time for renewal, your deceased loved ones' advice will be purified. Trust me; you'll know by trial and error when this occurs.

****

Wow! That is one great big spiritual Family we are connected to by the energy of Source. The discussion of it is a lot to digest. So, this may be a very good moment to take a break from reading and communicate with anyone, in any of the described spiritual groups. Here is some meditative guidance.

Sit still, and breathe deeply in and out for a minute or two. Try breathing in for 5 seconds, hold for 5 seconds, and release over 5 seconds; in through the nose; out through the mouth. Try to focus only upon your breathing for the time being. Close your eyes as you continue this breathing. When your mind is quieted, begin to imagine your very own sacred meeting place. This may be any combination of land, sea, sky, or other personally soothing images. Fill it with anything you wish to give comfort to its scene. After you are comfortably settled in, invite any of your many spiritual friends to join with you. Talk or just be together for 2-3 minutes. Finally, when you feel so very loved and refreshed, you can return to taking a look at the Divine Journey we are all on.

PART TWO

The Spiritual Being's Journey

The New World

We are, by essence, spiritual beings living within a physical body within a material environment. This was a choice each of us made at one time, with the intention of expressing God's 100% Love in a new perimeter of energy. Just before our time travel began, we co-created with Source a personal divine purpose and plans to advance it within a physical experience which we named "Earth." Agreed upon family, friends, and a lifetime of people, places, and events were set in motion to help develop our desire with lessons of all kinds along our way. With everything carefully selected and in order, our physical birth-day commenced.

With our physical transition, a tangible life dimension, filled with a variety of intricate material possessions, became our altered state of being. To help us adapt to the experience of our physical body, it was imbued with a Mind and the Five

Sense organs. The Mind (brain) provides us the functional ability to reason, think, feel, perceive, judge, desire, and remember. The Sense organs enhance, as well as protect, our physicality by relaying information from the outer world to appropriate places within our body's nervous system through general and specific neurons of the eyes, ears, tongue, skin, and nose.

These two amazing groups of human faculties, the Mind and the Senses, make it easier to understand why we live without spiritual recall for most of our earthly time. With all the wonder and accessibility of material goods and services, we actually are, as the saying goes, "living the dream." Yet, as we progress within each year of our earthly presence, two important shifts continue to take place.

The first is we become increasingly uncomfortable living by intellectual response alone; i.e., something always seems to be missing in our physical experiences and learned habits. This fogginess stems from relying solely upon mental references and responses. Also, we fill this mental library with perceptions gleaned from other "voices" such as, parents, teachers, neighbors, friends, media, and social systems; indeed, the entire human race that surrounds us (collective environment). This ongoing collection combines, whether we are attentive to it or not, with previous data and resides within our subconscious mind. From there, we execute choices to feel, speak, act, or react. Each choice builds the life of the physical body's personality or self-image (Ego), but not necessarily the spiritual being's life force. Nonetheless, as long as we are residing in a bodily form, in a physical dimension, Ego is very reliable.

The second gradual shift happens because our True Spirit continues to stir us to recall our holy intention of coming to this dimension in the first place. We feel this recurring nudge throughout our physical life cycle whether we respond to it or not. Because your Spirit is from the Source of Light, Love, and Truth, the voice of Spirit is gentle, patient, and kind. It is that ethereal essence within each of us which offers repeated inspiration, encouragement and synchronistic moments to arouse our spiritual course. The more we practice heart-centered listening, such as quiet meditation and sixth sensory energy, the more we discern this mystical whisper. From this awareness, we increasingly recall our divine purpose and act upon it measure by measure while on earth. We may do this consistently or sporadically along our way. There is no "right" or "wrong;" merely the opportunities to learn, practice, and teach. Because our spiritual contracts are individual, each human's life agenda and interacting participants will differ; and we may or may not complete our goal this time around.

What is true in all physical beings is that, within our lives on earth, we each come to a point where we intuitively know our travel here is complete. It is then, consciously or subconsciously, that death to the physical experience begins by this underlying instinctive choice. At that point, just the same as packing up our energy to move here, we begin to shed what we have acquired here: goods, services, places, and people. Finally, we shed the weighty physical form containing us. Just like being born in *to*, moving day *out* begins.

While the foregoing transitions may seem incredible, the only permanent life form any of us possess is indiscernible energy. That energy is forever connected to One Source, and thereby to each and every life force. Within this divine energy, we may create distinct transformations into one dimension, multiple or parallel dimensions, or hang where we're at.

When I first discerned this eternal potential within me and others, my curiosity led me to study and serve in this world as a sixth sensory guide and spiritual medium. I included the study of angelology and direct angel communication. I was most open and favorable to angel-speak and happenings. I must admit, I continue to favor these delightful spirits. I do believe it was angel guidance which moved me to further my sensory abilities and connect people here with their deceased loved ones on the Other Side.

In that beginning, there were again new signs and symbols of communication to learn. Sometimes struggling to learn and to translate, I would give my frustration over to angels for answers. In one very intense exchange with my angels about the deceased, I asked quite a few questions: "Where did they go?" "Where are they now?" "What are they doing over there?" and "How can I reach them?" You hear me say many times over that Angels always respond to us when we ask. Here following is some of the beauty and mystery of death and dying, and the stages of life-after-life which the Angels shared with me in those days that followed.

Moving Day

First, the angels sweetly shared that the reference to "resurrection" means "from" the body not "of" the body. They wished to confirm there are no physical bodies flying overhead on the Other Side. Rather, to die is to shed. Within the shedding process, the last physical breath of the body is the peak of transformation. From this place, many experts describe the next step of the dying process as travel through a "tunnel" to reach a mysterious white light. This imagery likely results from the description of those who experience a near-death occurrence and return to record such happenings. More exactly, the angels assure me that such an impression is really the movement of the spirit (life force) passing through and letting go of the temporal, elongated body. The "light" is, of course, your own true brilliance or Source to which your spirit is returning and reshaping.

Next, the angels remind me that each spiritual being's earthly makeover is preceded by a divine contract of the length of stay, encounters, and life lessons to take place while on earth. Because each life agreement will vary, death will also be distinctive. When death is imminent, there may be a long illness, lingering hours, or alternatively, a sudden occurrence which begins the body's shedding. However, with each person's beginning of death, divine guidance and choice are present, and communication is taking place not only from the human-side voices but also from the departing person's angels, spirit guides and relatives on the Other Side.

During such guidance, some of us choose to release ourselves readily; while others stay in unconsciousness longer for desired spiritual discussion. The expression for that end-time in which we go in and out of our two different dimensions is often labeled "twilighting." A longer exploration for the dying person and their choices is known to us as a coma. Additionally, there are those of us who curiously, if briefly, travel out of the body with an ethereal cord attached during the final hours to get a closer look at the Other Side and hear those voices up close and clearly. If any such person then chooses to travel back and revive into the declining physical body, the spiritual stopover is explained as a "near-death experience."

In the complete process, once bodily death is certain, many refer to the lifeless body as the moment of that person's "transition." This is very appropriate inasmuch as the word implies "change" or "transformation" and honors the Spirit's continuing life. My dialogue with my angels continued on as I asked again, "What next?" "Where are they?"

The Healing Pod

Upon each Spirit's return Home, the Sweet One (a name angels use) is welcomed into a spiritual "healing pod." We may think of this first after-death experience as similar to after-birth on earth. When we are newborn, there are no decisions to be made; only celebration; and love, care, and attention abound. Likewise, it is so within the spiritual healing pod. Newly arrived Sweet Ones are surrounded by their guardian angels, shared angels, spirit guides, and inner circle of friends and relatives. Jesus, Mary, and other Ascended Masters along with the Archangels are also present to cradle the returned holy ones in Love. God is present to all. This initial return Home is a period of incubation without stress or movement; free of all human awareness or remorse. It is a time of seeing beautiful images of universal spiritual growth before any individual conferences begin. The return of the spiritual beings to the healing pod is experienced by all who die from the physical body and its material experience.

The above revelation may give rise to concern about the holiness and fairness of the afterlife healing pod. Does this mean it is also a welcome place for deceased who have acted out evil, or at a minimum done little good in the physical world? While such alarm is validly human, it is only that: human. Don't forget each person on earth is first and foremost a spiritual being. All on earth left Home to create within a material space. This physical world or universe is comprised of co-opposites. A few simple examples are dark/light, large/small, high/low, hot/cold, and of course, love/hate. Clearly, we could not comprehend or name any one thing happening without the knowledge of its opposite. In this same regard, our own choices on earth are measured against unwanted values or opposites.

And so, it is true. Every spiritual being on earth will have a physical death; and all spiritual beings will return Home, beginning with the healing pod. For now, be grateful knowing that you have one of the "good parts" while you are here. Also, remember that any human being's negative behavior or extreme malevolence on earth comes from a physical person, and not from his or her divine Spirit. It is the divine Spirit, and only the divine Spirit, which returns Home. God will restore each as needed after its earthly journey.

The 5 Stages of Afterlife

In one of my many conversations with the angels, I asked about the Sweet Ones' spiritual existence on Return once they leave the healing pod. I know we return Home with the energy and imprints from our physical life of jobs, interests, and people connections. I did not know clearly what we do with these learned experiences once we are on the Other Side. Is there any plan over there, or do we just all "hang out" together nonchalantly? I hear my angels giggle at some of my musings, but I always trust in their response. My asking about what goes on after the renewed spirits leave the healing pod was unwavering.

One day thereafter, the angels spoke to me in one voice saying, "sit down and listen closely, we're going to tell you about the 5 Stages of Afterlife." I reached for a pen and paper to be at my side as our first session began. Following is the design of life after life shared with me in those conversations with the angels.

They began confirming the existence of the healing pod. Each deceased person (now spiritual being) remains in the healing pod according to his or her needs in that present moment. Some of the things which may affect the length of stay are the circumstances of the spirit's departure from the body and/or lingering memories of the physical life's hurts or disappointments, which are fresh in the emotional aura. Some spirits may require a longer period of "hugging" to restore confidence that all is well. There is no competition in the healing pod, and no Spirit is pressured to move on. Each "arrival," along with their guardian angels and familial greeters, will know when the rest and recreation (R & R) is sufficient. The moment of leaving this happy "group healing" will be obvious. It is then, from the warmth, welcoming, and cuddling of Return, the Sweet One begins five restoring stages, named The 5 Stages of Afterlife. They are:

Surprise, Concern, Attunement, Acceptance, and Bliss

These stages of Afterlife, while designed in an orderly framework, are not necessarily fixed stopovers. Any Sweet One may visit the middle three stages "to and fro" for the duration of lingering physical memory and emotions needing release. Some of the recurring thoughts, hurts, or unattended desires include perceived accomplishments or disappointments, addictive habits, or energetic pulls from people left behind – good, bad, or indifferent. No matter how frequent the back and forth occurs, the only purpose of having these heavenly stages is to wholly restore the spiritual being's awareness of God's pure Love, Light, and Power from which it emanates. Let's take a closer look at what happens in each stage.

Surprise

As we curiously wander from the healing pod, we enter the spiritual stage of "Surprise." The angels call this stage of new life "Surprise" because it is an occasion of overwhelming, indescribable delight. Here, the Sweet One is restored to witnessing the magical energy and beauty of all celestial possibilities which were forgotten long ago when a bodily experience was chosen. In a clear and wordless place, panoramic views of amazingly colorful scenes, joyfully entertaining sounds, tastes, and sensations created with God's love and vibration are presented as in a movie without end. I call this the "Yes I AM" place, because it is here that the Sweet Ones are shaken from the humanly acquired belief in limitation. It is here each returning Spirit's divine ability and expansion are reflected. And it is here those returning Spirits begin to recall the All.

Surprise is the first stage entered by Sweet Ones, and its delight also encourages playfulness. Loved ones on earth may feel the deceased loved one's newfound mischievousness in the form of interrupting sounds and inexplicable movements, sometimes called "bumps in the night." This is not the easiest Stage for you, or a medium, to message directly with the deceased loved one because, as you might guess, he or she is in a place of carefree distraction. Also, the magnificence they engage in is unavailable to our present physical understanding.

One thing is certain: it is most common for the newly arriving Sweet Ones to become so excited about what they "see" in this Stage, that they will wish to share it with one of us near or dear but yet on earth. Names are called out as they add "look at this!" You may feel such a call to you in the form of an energy pull; some examples are turning your head to look in a different direction and not knowing why, feeling the pores on your arms tingle, or hearing a piercing ring in the ear. There are also those of us who faintly hear our names called and ask someone near if they addressed us. It is very common to miss these faint connections, but they are within your sixth sensory reach.

Concern

This stage of Afterlife may be visited more frequently than the others. The first visit to this stage arises following a call out to others on earth to share in the magnificence present within the stage of Surprise. It is that instant when the newly freed spirit becomes aware that physical people, places, and things are no longer alongside or within reach. Questions begin such as: "How did I get here?" "Why didn't he/she come too?" "Is he/she okay?" These are quickly followed by something similar to, "Did I get everything done while I was there?" The Stage of Concern is a spiritual slide viewer of sorts, comfortable for magnifying earthbound people and moments in answer to lingering questions. Some reference this as a "life review," but it is much more.

We develop cords of astral energy to material places, persons, and events while we are enacting on earth. We also develop memories of loves, joys, sorrows, and habits, to name a few. When that energy is not cut (released) during the physical life period, it is carried over within the deceased one's emotional aura. There it may vibrate a satisfying sensation (a love shared), or it may arouse additional questions which slow the new Spirit's sacred journey. Whichever arises, when the new Spirit is in a stage of Concern, the soul's energy is drawn back to earth time, and it is not engaging in timeless space. For some individuals, this stage may include a stir to meddle again in that life left behind. I call these clinging spirits "ghosts."

The stage of Concern is available for the new Spirit to see leftover attachments to the material world – persons, places, things – and to build confidence to release them for his higher good. Depending upon the life lived and the person's creations and miscreations alike, this may be more simply said than achieved. So, it is from here at this stage, where the angels escort the spiritual being into the stage of Attunement. Think of this next stage as "spiritual education" and/or "spiritual career guidance" offered by spirit guides and heavenly experts.

Attunement

Attunement is a heavenly bridge from past life experiences to contemplative choice and future creation. It is a place of retreat where spirits may seek sacred adjustments to their new life form and intention. Within the love and quiet of this stage, material world residues and perceived longings are addressed, such as people, places, happenings, and perceived completion of that previous life's purpose. A library of not only the very recent past but of all experienced lives is looked at and discussed with celestial counselors. Some religions on earth mention this spiritual phase as a place of "final judgment." It is, however, a cosmic point which is anything but "final" for visitation and processing of the soul's creations past, present, or imaginable.

In Attunement, God's presence is experienced as fluid divine guidance, not static judgment. The guidance and explanations within this spiritual surrounding are presented by angels and Ascended Masters. The spirits of every esteemed scholar, musician, writer, singer, dancer, and all performing artists who have ever lived in the material world are present within this phase. The Sweet Ones may hang out with these renowned experts and absorb, not merely witness their valued talents.

Anytime a spiritual being visits or revisits Attunement, yearnings are unraveled, worry is dismissed, and powerful new skills become available. It is also here that heavenly career choices abound to which anyone and everyone may apply. Competition is stilled, and advancement is shared and applauded. For some, the option of reincarnation or walk-in value is discussed. And without exception, it is within this stage that volunteers are trained according to evident talent and past professions to assist the "incoming."

In summary, Attunement is a spiritual place where incremental adjustments raise confidence and increase comfort in the renewed life form. It is here (the angels tell me) where, with each visit, more clarity of and participation in the Divine "big picture" accelerates.

Acceptance

Acceptance is the stage of Afterlife wherein the Sweet Ones progressively release the label of "deceased;" embracing instead the reality of spiritual origin and its continuation. This is to say they stop keeping one foot in each world. The uninterrupted connection with God is remembered and revitalized. Lingering attachments to the physical body and its atmosphere are freely cleansed. Images and memories of the mortal experience are now understood by the spiritual being to be but one of its many eternal stories. As such, they are saved in the Sweet One's ethereal aura for reference and new adventures. Thankfully, the rhythm and strength of relationships with others on earth are also kept in the aura, available for our continuing dialogue.

Because divine vision is restored in the Stage of Acceptance, the spiritual being's next sacred evolution is now comfortably decided. The Sweet One's personal angelic guardians (see "guardian angels") convene with the Spiritual being to assist any advanced transition. For some of us, this may be another material experience, and for others not. It is healing to understand this is a stage of absolute tranquility, not judgment;

and free will abounds. A good analogy for this period is a Closing Date.

Lifetimes past and experiments enjoyed will direct each spiritual being's choice. For those accepting another physical life, the challenges of time and grounded vibration will return, and the previous physical memory will be erased to afford a different life story. For those deciding to advance creation celestially, heavenly guides and masters will take those spirits in hand as they begin their way. For all returning spirits, it is within the Stage of Acceptance that as spiritual beings we reinvest fully in our True Origin and unending, divine potential. We fully recognize that Love is all that's real and forever expressed by our lives' breath.

Bliss

Bliss is the stage of supreme blessedness. It is the place where our True Spirits will overflow with a deep and uninterrupted sense of Gratitude and Joy and nothing less. In this celestial stage, spiritual beings enjoy the peaceful stillness that human hearts chase life after life. Here, pursuits are paused, and all spirits vibrate with the ecstasy which one Divine Life presents.

God, and only God, is experienced. Love is absolute. One Breath and one imagination are revered. It is truly the "view from above," where the original omnipotent, holy nature of all life forms is remembered and permeates all energy and senses. The angels say this stage is the one which many generations on earth have only been able to refer to as "Namaste." Now a reality, Bliss is the stage where Sweet Ones are at last filled with the understanding of the place within each of us which is of Love, of Truth, of Light, and of Peace.

PART THREE

Conversations with Heaven

The Wish to Connect

Every living human being holds within its subconscious, a memory of its original Divine Origin. This stored truth stirs occasional yearnings to link to more than our present material experience. From time to time, we will search for mystical means to describe events which cannot be mentally resolved. The most common trigger to this unusual pursuit will arise with the physical death of a loved one. This is because all things comfortably shared through our familiar five senses are brought to a halt. We long for another opportunity "to have" and "to hold" each other. Our mental being seems to block any hope of relief, and we, therefore, look to develop our supernatural kinship.

In addition to the need to reconnect with deceased familial beings, most of us develop a curiosity to connect with other spiritual beings of which stories tell. These include saints, angels, and spirit guides – all who emanate from God just as we do. We search because our Divine connection to them remains subliminal. Indeed, this why we pray. Likewise, this is why the spirits' world of energy is always drawn to and has a path to touching ours. An example of an impulsive inter-world exchange is any moment when a person sees a glimpse of movement past the corner of an eye, and upon turning, sees nothing. This is most often a traveling spirit passing by or one attempting to communicate directly. (Think, Angels!)

There are many questions my clients ask about connecting with spiritual beings, such as angels or their deceased loved ones. Some of the most common are: "Can they see me?" "Can they hear me?" "How can I reach them?" I wish I could say the connecting from side to side of our two worlds is as simple as speaking aloud to any voice recognition device. Despite human advancements, it is simply not true.

One of the challenges in reaching each other from both sides of heaven (cosmos) arises due to the variance of the energetic vibration each plane (being) gives out. All on the physical plane emit a slow, mentally processed vibe. In contrast to this, all in the spirit world give out high-speed spontaneous impressions. Spirits are disengaged or freed from everything dense and physical and this includes the need to articulate as we know it. In addition, the ethereal being's vibration cannot be seen with our naked-eye; and this lessens the ability to interpret messaging with our familiar five senses of hearing, touch, taste, sight, and smell. While these senses are beautiful and will support our interworld communication, a newly accepted vernacular must also be developed between us and those who are fully translucent.

Another obstacle for we humans, when wishing to get in touch with the supernatural world, is the significance our mental being gives to material locations. Because our mortal awareness is all things physical, we attach that narrow mental understanding to the whereabouts of those unseen or deceased. In particular, we give names to possible locations of the physically departed such as "heaven," "with God," "a better *place*," (or the opposites) and so forth.

But this material perception distracts us from incoming *spiritual* signals. So, as you yearn, try to remember the only move the Sweet Ones (deceased) have made from their past to present experience is the shedding of the physical form. The bodily release is what changed the density of their energy. With the heightened, lighter, faster energy, they are no longer in need of stationary locations; rather, they experience fluidity within an unlimited atmosphere. Comparatively, our physical (bodily) energy is heavy and stabilized by our defined mass and surroundings. This difference of frequency between worlds is not impenetrable, but for interworld dialogue, it does call for adjustment in the wavelengths from both directions. Our effort on earth is to lighten (lighten up!) our energy vibration, and for celestial beings to lower theirs (get grounded).

Sending and Receiving

The initial step for humans wishing to connect with the spirit world is to nurture a desire and willingness to communicate beyond that which is physically apparent (normal). Since our birth into our physical being, we've become comfortable with dismissing anything we cannot see or mentally support as existent. For example, when we look around a room, we see the walls, floor, ceiling, and objects or things within or on them. While we breathe the air within, rarely do we consciously notice it. Still, if you think about it, we must be subtly aware there is more than what is seen because we build windows! Of course, in our physical awareness, we look through those windows for yet more matter common to the human sense of awareness. But the Sweet Ones who are now bodiless spirits, no longer fit our material perception. So, to connect with them, we need to build a *paranormal* window into their new place which they can use to be in contact with us.

Much like opening a physical window, we open it with pressure; but now we apply our sixth sensory strength to the unseen pane. In doing so, we expand beyond our human perception of boundaries and engage in psychic awareness. Practice will perfect it, and there are easy exercises to move your ability forward. A few of these simple workouts include regularly meditating; clearing the spiritual power centers (chakras) within the body; increasing the five senses' daily stimuli, dietary changes, and of course, prayer. As you learn to use your sixth sensory ability, it may be helpful to work with an accomplished spiritual mentor or medium.

It's good to know there is a given jumpstart for joining with your loved Sweet Ones. All physical beings on earth nurture particular and shared feelings throughout their lifetime. These sensations are stored in the emotional aura and attach to our conscious activities. Unless we purposefully dismiss any of these feelings *before* we die, which is not usually the case, these sensations are carried over into our new heavenly aura. From there, they may be reviewed or stimulated at any time. For those of us still on earth, this means the

Sweet Ones may indeed send or receive a signal through the rise of emotions still mutually in place.

The rhythm and clarity of the celestial's signal are identical to the degree of passion for the same stimulus known (thing or person) while living on earth. For instance, while your deceased loved one can no longer sit at the table with you for any of those family spaghetti dinners, often when you enjoy this familiarity, you will attract your Sweet One's intangible presence. You may even find yourself and family suddenly speaking about that person. Similar to this example, if shared meals were important to a deceased loved one, you might find yourself noticing a picture or smell of a favorite meal signaling the nearness of his/her presence to yours. I call these the "hello" or "just thinking of you" messages.

The Sweet Ones' messaging is infinite in creativity and delivery, but their choice is usually specific enough to ultimately grab your attention. Be mindful of previous signs, symbols, and actions you once shared, because they will cherish it equally and make it their "pen." Here's an example:

> *I was visiting in my kitchen with my great-niece. We were chatting across the kitchen island with each other. On a side note, my great-niece, now an adult, was born quite a*

few years after her grandfather had died in an accident, and the two had never personally met. However, I knew him and visited my sister and him in their home oftentimes so many years ago. Now, as my great-niece and I shared talk and laughter, I found myself mixing our cocktails, nonchalantly stirring one glass after the other with my index finger. As I realized my poor manners, I looked up and explained to her, "Oh sorry, that's something I absentmindedly do now and then because I once found your grandfather doing the same in his kitchen when he was overwhelmed with his house guests' peculiar drink requests. There he was in his kitchen with a line of glasses; mixing, finger stirring and tasting. I remember how funny I thought it was as I called his name out to interrupt his effort!"

I went on to tell my great-niece, that since that time long ago every now and then I find myself nonchalantly stirring in that same manner; and whenever I catch myself, I do one more swirl then point my finger to the sky, and say, "Hi, Frank!" My great-niece smiled genuinely, but it's what I saw next which brought me a pleasant chill. As I looked up to smile back at her, I saw her grandfather standing right beside her. He was intently gazing on his beautiful granddaughter's face, displaying his one-of-a-kind grin along with sparkling tears. I could feel the love and great longing before his vision disappeared. Most naturally I passed his message of love along to her. And even though I have no glass before me right now, as I share this story, I pause and point my finger to the sky once more with expectation of a smile returned.

So, you see, the fleeting moments we share with each other in this life will become somewhat of a "doorbell" to each other in altered states every time we tell the story!

The Sweet Ones are translucent and fluid. In my experience, they will appear as they wish or favor. Think of them engaging with a curiosity equal to or greater than that of our childhood, adding in new supernatural skills. They love to have fun! They are no longer ill or handicapped or aged; rather, they are free to conjure up the "look" they love best and adorn it with the things they enjoyed most. For instance, they usually pick their preferred age when they appear and not necessarily the age last known on earth. They choose conditions and clothing they deem to be their best personal signature while on earth: a particular hat, shirt, ring, or other things. They may act out a favorite pastime or speak words related to the work they enjoyed. Sometimes they utilize body language such as crossing their arms, tapping a forehead, or any type of customary gesture. They continue to enjoy family-friend celebrations and will still attend many of yours; so, when you write out invitations, try writing one with their name upon it.

One of the Sweet Ones who would be connecting in a session to his mother appeared earlier on to me. He asked me to buy two yellow roses for the meeting. When the day arrived, he again spoke to me, asking that I not give them to her right away, but rather when their time together was complete. Because his death was accidental, he wished to first clarify what happened on the day he parted. During our session, he did this first, and I relayed his words to my client. Then he said, 'Actually, Mom, I must tell you, now that I am here, I truly love it and am really comfy." He added, 'It was all a bit scary for me in the physical world . . . I do miss you, Daddy, and Andy . . . but I just want you to know that I'm totally healthy and enjoying this place!'

Then he showed himself to me as a boy with light-colored, tousled hair and a hat loosely worn to the side. His mother confirmed it was him because he always wore that hat. Next, he asked if his mom would turn and hug him even if she could not see. After I relayed his request, this beautiful, courageous mother stood up, turned around and walked a few steps. She outstretched her arms and without a further thought encircled them around her son's spiritual body. I could see them both as they held each other for the longest time. When they completed their silent loving, her son gently pulled his energy back, beginning to take leave.

I then remembered the two yellow roses hidden away and gave them to my client. I explained the untold story of his asking me to buy them for her. With gently falling teardrops, she said, "We have a garden in our home in France, and the garden is filled with yellow roses. After he died, it was there that I first felt him." With a final message for that day, I shared as her son said, "Whenever you go there, Mom, I will be there too."

The above story is one of a deceased son in the heavenly Stage of Acceptance, and not only his mother's deep love but also her knowingness and trust. With practice, you will develop your own knowingness and heighten your clear sight (clairvoyance) with each encounter you undertake. Make it your intention to respect energy beyond physical barriers and be open to receiving it. Start by giving credit to those times you find yourself turning your head before thinking about it; seeing "nothing;" and yet feeling someone was near. You can believe a spirit did brush by you – some known, some unknown. Anytime you become aware of one of these spiritual nudges, it's a good habit to acknowledge with a short greeting: "hi," "how're you doing?" or if unwelcomed: "move on."

Here is another piece of magic toward enjoying your new connection with those in Spirit. Try to await or select positive feelings before linking. Practice sitting in silence and slowing down your mental grip on anguish (or anger) by purposefully selecting positive sentiments from your emotional field such as laughter, pride, serenity, inspiration, and, of course, Love. Engage your five senses to see, hear, feel, taste, and smell those many moments. Once you have locked in on the delightful feelings, ask aloud for your loved one to rejoin with you in this joy-filled impression, *in the present moment*. Every one of us is drawn to each other's expressions of happiness, and the Sweet Ones are no different in this way.

Admittedly, being joyful in the beginning stages of physical loss is a huge challenge. The closer the relationship on earth was, the more severe the separation anxiety may be. This is true for both "Sides." Be assured the Sweet Ones miss touching you and hearing your voice as much as you are pining for shared moments with them. However, if we allow our intense longing to remain in our focus, both Sides remain stuck with one foot in each world. The newly deceased are suspended between celestial grandeur and the afterlife stage of Concern. Likewise, an underlying heaviness of your heart chakra is not conducive to your emotional well-being and may affect your physical health as well. Here is my personal story:

> *One of my darkest times was the death of my father Bill and the overwhelming grief which followed. I was missing him so much day-to-day that oftentimes I found myself ending my workday, sitting in a chair at home, and staring blankly out the window in continuing disbelief. He truly was the sole person in my life who greatly understood me, and I was stunned and terrified to continue my life's journey without his intuitive perception. Each night for nearly two years forward, I would find myself in astral travel with him when I lay down to rest. We would walk our favorite beach; I would present my day's concerns, and he would offer his familiar and very wise advice. I would apply that advice within my waking hours, and it*

always rung true. However, each time I awakened from our closeness in astral travel, his physical death reared its head in detail once more. Words such as, "oh, that's right, you're not here," would fall from my voice. Most concerning was that my depression was ruling my daily interactions and overshadowing the amazing life all around me.

I made a choice to visit a psychic intermediary to present my case. I asked her to contact my father and see if he was okay; and, if so, ask him if he would let go of our connection because I must do the same for the time being. When the healer told me he was well, happy, and understood, I became soaked within my tears. This "letting go" seemed as difficult as the everyday grief.

And when I returned home, there was an evident level of silence all around me. Hesitantly, I said aloud, "thank you, Dad." I put his picture out of sight for a time, and in the days and months forward I was able to revitalize my attention to my own life. It was joyful, good, and moving forward. Somehow, I felt assured the same was true for him. Our nighttime travel ceased.

Another year passed as each of our energies cleansed in delight. Then our amazing reunion occurred!

I turned up the radio one afternoon hearing the song "Unchained Melody." Something pulled me to look toward it, hearing the words, "Oh my love, my darling." I looked over at the radio and there between it and me stood my father, Bill. What was new was I distinctly saw him in this moment of conscious awareness. I saw his physical appearance from head to toe: his beautiful blue eyes, loving cup ears, long arms, and piano fingers. He wore his favorite color of yellow shirt – perfectly pressed as always. Reaching out his hand to me, he bid me to dance. I returned the reach and felt his hand finger to finger. I even felt the cool metal of the flat-headed ring he always wore. And most certainly, I could smell the aroma of his Old Spice cologne. We danced and held each other's eyes. Smiles turned to grins. Then as we continued, I took a risk. I began tilting myself backward and said aloud, "Catch me, Dad." It was something we always did when I was a little girl and a would-be-ballerina. I let myself go further toward the floor, and suddenly there was his arm catching me, then lifting me back up. We finished our dance and touched index-to-index fingers while smiling at each other. I could finally say with joy, "I love You,

Daddy!" and he nodded his head in kind.

This time I was not afraid when we parted and was more assured that he was not so far away. Now and again, since those moments shared, "Unchained Melody" will play by random somewhere and he will return. Sometimes I play the song and invite him. Either way, forever it became our song, although it never before was.

It is a good idea to gradually disengage from the emotional connection we hold for each other as soon as possible after the death for a temporary period of time. This will give emotional cleansing to the important spiritual channels (sixth sensory) which are necessary to reconnect the relationship from both "Sides."

In the beginning, after my father's physical death, my unrestrained grief kept me in a recurring state of emotional anguish. Simultaneously, my hopeless feelings repeatedly called my father's spirit into the afterlife stage of Concern. With such a connection, we were both "spinning our wheels" against joyful progress. I'm not suggesting you forget or deny your gloomy or depressed emotions, but I am asking you to realize you *own* your emotions and may choose or change them as you wish at any time. And, if you regularly clear and recreate your emotional field, I promise you too will enjoy many a "dance."

The Sweet Ones, as stated, are surrounded by angels who soothe the new spirits' separation anxiety within the afterlife stages of Attunement and Acceptance. For those of us here, the challenge is to lighten, not so much the "heart," as the dense mental energy attending the trauma of a person's physical departure. It is a very sound practice to choose a time each day to *purposefully* quiet your internal mental chatter. This is a healthy practice called meditation. Meditation does not have to be a guided application with a headset or within a class. In its simplest form, it is available to you at any time, with any length you choose. All you have to do is stop any frantic or fidgety activity and be still. Here's a simple exercise to help your practice:

Sit quietly and focus only on your breathing: in 5 counts, hold 5 counts, and out 5 counts. Do this for a minute or so. After that, bring to mind the comfortable and satisfying place your imagination created earlier on ("sacred place"). Continue to add everything and anything soothing to you within it. Think of a simple gesture, such as a finger tracing the infinity sign. You will use your signing whenever you enter here.

As you rest within this magical place, look around and up and down, and receive the love in every corner, base, or ceiling. There are many angels smiling over you eager to teach and provide answers.

Look to a particular doorway and see your angels coming toward you with colorful balloons in a basket, not yet filled with air. The angels extend the basket toward you and bid you to choose as many as you wish. In exchange for the balloons, the angels ask you to place all your tears, fears, and worries in the basket. The angels take the basket filled with all your heavy feelings and add them, one-by-one, into a nearby helium tank. Now it's your turn once more.

You walk over to the tank and fill each colored balloon you chose with the helium. Your angels tie the ends of each with a string and hand them back to you. Next, you see the ceiling above you in this sacred place, opening to a magnificent, infinite sky. You hear your angels softly say, "Let them go . . . let them go."

As you willingly release the strings, the balloons take a greater and greater flight. It is a beautiful, amazing flight which goes way beyond your reach until out of sight. But along its journey, you somehow realize that all the sorrow within each balloon is transmuted into Light. You feel a heightened sense of tranquility and joy knowing all of your perceived troubles and fears are now gone.

Sit quietly and enjoy the fullness of the magical release for as long as you wish. Close your meditation by saying with love, "And so it is."

Learning Symbolism

One of the questions I often receive from my clients is, "Do you think it could be a sign?" There are many signs and symbols in our material world, and your angels, guides, and deceased loved ones will use those most common to your attention. Here are some of the common symbols within spiritual jargon which may appear to you in actuality, meditation, or dreams:

> Bouquets of flowers and particular colors; birthday cakes; candles; trophies or awards; rolled diplomas; birds; butterflies and hummingbirds; animals; coins or paper money; rainbows; a penny on the ground; a single feather on your walk; leaves randomly blowing toward you; the sound of water flowing; and almost all that is symbolic of nature.

The above is merely a quick reference, and there are, of course, many more physical signs the Sweet Ones will choose for messaging. For example, my husband's daughter treasured a little porcelain cow creamer, which was a gift we found for her at an oceanside art fair. She was so very sad when a friend knocked it off her kitchen counter, and it broke. While my husband and I spent a little time whenever we traveled looking for a replacement, we never found one. However, in the years after she died, porcelain knickknack cows began showing up now and then when I am shopping – although still no creamer. Each time this happens, I return her "hello," and even add, "I know, I know." Once there was an island display in a grocery store decorated at its four corners with cow balloons. I could truly hear her distinct giggle. I might add we receive other messages from her, but the recurring cows are among my favorite.

All of the above is to assure you the Sweet Ones will select material signs according to their previous earthly affection and newfound spiritual capability. They will use their angels' assistance, and your angels may even be the go-between. Some signs may be easily defined by you; others not so much. Spiritual messages may be scheduled or impromptu, directly to you, or by intermediary means. For instance, you may receive an unexpected bouquet from someone in the color or colors your deceased loved one favored or consistently gave to you. This occurs from "guided shopping" such as in the story of the mother, son, and yellow roses. Messaging may also occur when you are attracted to a new thing or place which seems to feel familiar – it could be part of the Sweet One's untold story. Or, you might meet someone at a gathering and notice cologne or another identifiable scent.

The reason a message for you may come through another person or medium is not because you are loved "less." Quite the contrary; you are loved very much and have been a little oblivious to the Sweet One's attempt to message you. Because I am an "easy contact," many times a determined Sweet One will raise my attention. I always pass the message along whenever I can. Have the courage to pass along messages you may receive for others no matter how small or silly it may seem at the time. Even a "hello" is very important to the sender.

Your first few messages from your Sweet Ones may be so spontaneous that they are a bit startling. Practice maintaining a sense of ease because the deceased loved ones do not want you to be afraid or upset. I have witnessed some readings wherein the sitter's tentativeness causes the Sweet One to temporarily pull back rather than upset the person. So, it is important you communicate to them, "It's okay; you can come." Acknowledge the celestial sender generally until you have more clarity. For example, say "thank you" when you feel an energy connection, even if you are unable to immediately identify the message itself, or who the spirit messenger is. You'll always have time to ask for additional illumination. Gratitude is the magnifier of all things, especially continuing relationships.

Another good practice is to have ready a sign or gesture familiar to the two of you; such as a wink, smile, or air kiss. Ask your angels to deliver it, requesting a "return receipt." Remember to ask for confirmation of the signs sent in either direction. In my experience, incoming spiritual signs and symbols will repeat three or more times in the weeks forward after the first notice. As you learn to believe in the material signals sent to you by your unseen spiritual family, it will seem normal to ask for more detail such as, "What are you trying to say to me?" The answer will take shape in the days ahead.

Next, it's good to recall spiritual beings love good etiquette as much as we enjoy our manners on earth. It's polite when you address the Sweet Ones to use their previously used name, rather than their association with you. One reason for this is the relationships we shared on earth with the Sweet Ones are likely a commonly named bond shared between many others at one time. Calling out "mom," "dad," "sweetheart," etc. may draw a crowd and confusion. And it truly is possible that your loved ones no longer recall the exact term depending on their afterlife stage. Names, however, follow us through and over.

Good manners for spiritual conversations also suggest we say, "excuse me," when we wish to interrupt the loved one to ask for more information. A final social practice is to be certain to invite, not demand, the presence of those you are trying to reach. Most all of these dear souls have newfound independence and will not respond to a perceived command. Still others suggest they have many things to do and "cannot talk" or still hold their earthly personality of busyness or distraction.

Enjoy practicing these new types of connections. The more you are willing to normalize a Sweet One's attempt to contact you, the clearer the next message or visit will be. So, pick up the penny at your feet and say, "hi." If the phone rings once, then stops, try saying, "Stay a little longer next time." If a light is flickering or your ears are ringing, say, "I know you're here, but I can't understand fully; please tell me more." Of course, you can always add, "I love you" and blow a kiss! Keep up the practice of voiced appreciation when signs of spiritual visitors are near (or voice your dismissal when the feeling is not good). Remain patient in learning the "talk." Finally, but always, follow this simple acronym to improve your altered form of reception: **T.R.U.S.T.** (**T**o **R**eceive **Y**ou **S**top **T**hinking).

Fine-Tuning Our Good Senses

In our present material body, our need for union or re-union with others is primarily founded upon our five senses; in particular that of touch. It should be easy to understand the root of our panic and grief when a person dies is the lost sense of touch or "skin hunger" for that human. However, we have not really lost our ability to see, hear, or feel them; rather, we have numbed the very senses available to us with which do so. Throughout our comings and goings on earth, we have become accustomed to placing our sensory ability on automatic pilot. This is to say we allow our senses to arouse us or color our experiences more often than we prompt them to awaken and attend to us.

Expanding the manner in which our five senses influence our moments will, in turn, strengthen our sixth sensory (spiritual) ability. There is indeed something so true about the phrase, "*Stop* and smell the flowers." Consider extending this "stop" exercise often to the other four senses as well. For instance, stop and listen closely. How many and what type sounds do you hear? Stop and describe the many things you see around you: the shapes, colors, dimensions. Stop and slowly feel a material surface or hold an item in your hand until your awareness raises to its texture. Stop and allow your palate to linger a little longer in absorbing anything you taste. Interchange the five senses as you explore anything your mind can hold, including your heart's desires. *What does it look like? Taste like? Smell like? Sound like? Feel like?* These exercises are enjoyable, not difficult. The biggest benefit is that the more we give our five senses and our imagination a daily workout, the greater the possibility to raise our super-consciousness to *The All* becomes.

In addition to exercising the five senses, there is another method to nourish your sixth sensory ability: purposely set aside time for daydreaming. Although most often implied by observers to be a time-wasting detachment, daydreaming is, in fact, the mind's natural ability to imagine! And, because we are in essence extrasensory beings, it is more than okay to detach from our immediate physical surroundings and substitute visionary travels from time to time. Indeed, daydreaming strengthens our spiritual or clairvoyant sight (the mind's eye) and fosters trust in our Divine connection. The more often we entertain our mental desires and visualize the wonder of "what ifs," the more we open up to our True Spirit and the ability to believe beyond what we physically recognize. From there, signs and symbols of our inter-world communication become familiar and clear.

I hope you can guess, allowing time for divine imagination will quickly advance your psychic abilities for connecting with spiritual partners; such as angels and Sweet Ones. Begin to bless your daydreams and give dedicated time to roam within them fully. The more you are able to dream, the fuller your spiritual glossary and the magic of it will become.

> *Whatever you can do,*
> *or dream you can,*
> *Begin it*
> *Boldness has genius, power and*
> *Magic in it."*
> ~ Goethe

PART FOUR

The Present Moment

The Fading Memory

Living on earth – a material plane – and in a material body is each human's choice for the present moment. We believe ourselves to be primarily physical, mental beings, hereon chasing something of a higher and more eternal consciousness. However, we are, by origin, wholly and purely energy beings emanating from eternal Love, Light, and Intelligence. In fact, the term "children of God" reflects our faint memory of the everlasting, authentic life form we have enjoyed. From our place in holiness, and from the highest form of energy, we created a transition of our purely spiritual selves into a mortal experience.

Our intention in creating this life form shift was to underscore and expand our knowingness of God's 100% Divine Magnificence in a new world. To begin our spiritual project, we created with Source a temporary place of all things dense in energy and corporeal in desire, including the body, lower mind, and ego. And as mentioned earlier, each of us brought to earth a unique outline for our personal, material adventure. We agreed to learn while we teach so that we might keep expanding. We chose family, friends, and many encounters to support or challenge us in the new life. As difficult as it is to believe, we even chose duration. As a final touch, we outlined our new format with our emotional aura to give color. It was indeed an amazing Plan.

Misfortunately, upon arriving, the memory of this Divine Awareness faded from recollection. Much like any traveler in a new land, we were pleasantly surprised with the magnificence of our designed surroundings. The many tangible things of earth set before our now physical senses turned out to be very attractive, entertaining, and subtly distracting. Moreover, as long as we are in the physical body, this fascination with the tangible continues. Coincidentally, as we remain absorbed in our material understandings, we develop what the angels call spiritual amnesia. While there is nothing unreasonable about using our material surroundings and inventions to favor and support us here on earth, it's all rather flipped in priority. Thus, underlying our adventures, we are experiencing confusion about our present location, and just exactly what it is we set out to do. We wonder about our true purpose in being here; and amidst our many ways, there is subtle longing to restore sacred clarity and sequence. Where do we start and what might be a meaningful life path to recovery?

"You Are Here"

City points of interest maps and retail shopping directories use a little arrow with the reference "You Are Here" to help you more easily choose your day's course. Wouldn't it be wonderful to enjoy a similar arrow in front of our eyes along this earthly journey to guide us to the best choices for our experience?

It may amaze you to hear every one of us has a similar location pointer within reach with every breath we take. It's called "True Spirit." True Spirit is that pure Light, Love, and Intelligence radiating from God within your fundamental spiritual self. It cannot be broken; it will not die; indeed, it connects you, me, and the All. You can find it and check-in with it any time you wish. All you need do is look into the mirror of your physical eyes, place your hand over your physical heart, and take time to ask, "What does my Spirit say?" While face-to-face is the most stimulating, you may place your hand over your heart and ask anywhere, at any time you wish. Divine Intelligence will always be sparked. The more often you ask, the more finely-tuned the inner (psychic) hearing becomes, which, in turn, recognizes the "feel-good" options available to serve your highest good while on earth. How great is that!

Up till now, most of our earthly mapping has been founded upon our mental awareness and judgments. We support our everyday path and choices by referring to our present material environment. With this human approach, we have grown accustomed to navigating our lives by a course of physical and mental perceptions, actions, and reactions. For the most part, it is a reliable approach in terms of cause and effect. But when we rely *only* upon this method, without checking-in with our intrinsic divine spirit, we will periodically feel disappointed, unfulfilled, unclear, and discouraged; often followed by stints of depression.

Wouldn't it be more attractive to awaken every day knowing you will be living easily and effortlessly? You can enjoy exactly this when you make a habit of relying upon inner guidance from your divine Spirit. True Spirit will always give the sensation of delight with every material step on earth you create. You have angels all around you who are eager to help you tap into the energy of this one True Spirit. As mentioned above, all you have to do is ask, listen, and act. To strengthen your reception of divine guidance, remember to love and acknowledge this God-connection every day. Do this with mirrored eyes affirming to your Self:

> I AM a Trace of Heaven
> Holy Spirit, Decide for Me

From "Here" On

The phrase "present moment" remains a commonplace reference in our everyday dialogue. This is because it is useful in defining our place of mental focus. An example is heard within guided meditations such as, *"try to stay* in the present moment," or *"just return to"* the present moment. These are invitations to purposefully hold attention on anything you can perceive <u>for the first time</u>; rather than process the past or speculate the future. More simply said, it means to stop thoughts and allow the mind to recover in silence and empty space. What possible purpose could this forced effort have? The answer is "original creation." We give ourselves time to step away from internal mental chatter preventing it.

There is some research which suggests the mind processes more than 64,000 thoughts in a 24-hour period. Studies further believe most of those thoughts are replays of past moments or conjectures about the future. Whether they are joyful or not, it's important to know all of those replays and conjectures are static effort; that is, nothing is altered or new. The "past" is stationary, and the "future" is symbolic. The "present moment" is the only place wherein we access pure energy to move forward or perform work. It is a period of material time in which thoughts become action, either consciously or subconsciously. And, no matter what the number of daily thoughts actually is, we do know our subconscious memories and projected concepts are continuously downloading to our mental well-being.

So then, your angels invite you to really make an effort to notice those thoughts running through your mind throughout the minutes of the day. Regularly ask yourself, "What am I thinking *right now*?" As you consciously notice the ideas of your mind more and more, you'll learn to catch and release (verbalize: cancel-cancel-delete) those which are unfavorable to your happiness and calm. Increasingly, you'll find yourself nurturing more of those thoughts which support your best interest and bring them into action. Once again, referring back to the retail map or directory analogy, "You are Here." From "Here" travel wisely forward into the Present Moment.

There you will create the next step, and the next, and the next, to arrive at your planned destination; that is, the Source of your highest good and the highest good of all.

> *"The secret of health, for both mind and body, is not to mourn for the past, not to worry about the future, or not to anticipate troubles, but to live in the present moment wisely and earnestly."* ~ Buddha

PART FIVE

Until We Meet Again

Human Resilience

No matter how many times we say or hear the word "death," and, no matter how many times we use the word to acknowledge our own mortality, our emotional response is contempt for the experience. We have attached to its event, or probable event, fear, sorrow, hopelessness, and even rip-off. We bundle this group of dark feelings into the word "grief." We endure other losses throughout our lives, but the loss by death is our greatest. It is, in a word, "awful." In any account of grief, is it possible to recolor the painful feeling into something lighter, brighter, and more positive when it rears its presence? Gradually, yes. We begin to move in this direction with a little better look into the underlying cause of our sorrow; in this case, death.

The simple definition of the word "death" means an "end." When the description "end" is attributed to the physical body, it means the breathing or life force *in such form* comes to a halt. The statement of this as a fact seems plain and harmless. Even so, without clear recollection of our fundamental spiritual nature, a material "death" is met only as a permanent conclusion of a being's *whole* life – a life we became dependent upon. This practiced emotional response to death is an unfortunate human misunderstanding; particularly as it relates to one's "whole life" and its endurance. In truth, only the earthly death is permanent; within it, the Spirit is mercurial and unending. As we accept this spiritual reality, we will see all physical deaths are only a *part* of one's life and not the whole. It is in our best health to live in this greater understanding that after the end of the body's life, a new beginning follows.

> *"One doesn't discover new lands*
> *without consenting to lose sight,*
> *for a very long time, of the shore."*
> ~Andre Gide

Human beings are very resilient. Certainly, throughout our lifetimes on earth, we execute many "ends," some as simple as a meal, a visit; others as engaging as schooling, housing, traveling, and career. When they end, we look forward to a new or different adventure. Yet, while these life interruptions and changes do carry some uneasiness; none seem as severe as the apprehension we attach to the body's death. This is because we perceive a threatening contrast.

When we end a situation or activity within our material life – even if it was forced upon us – we feel in control of what is next (choices to take). We are able to mentally map a new beginning; no matter what that may be. Relying on our intellect, we reason through available, *visible* options. On the other hand, the demise of the material body seems to deny us that authority. This is because at the moment the body ends, the new beginning is yet to be seen or known. Emotional upset is felt because we cannot single out the "next step" from where we stand. In this perceived helplessness, we seem to have lost all personal power.

Yet, even in our humanness, our personal power is always intact. In particular, the truth is no one dies without their consent. Whether we recall or not, we each made our own spiritual-mortal contracts before introducing our celestial selves into this form. Even if our awareness has become subtle, we are in charge of our present lives, even to the end. More in this regard, we could not possibly lose control over something we were never in charge of in the first place; which is another person's personal contract for his lifetime. Therefore, when those feelings of panic arise from death's experience, remember

with confidence other endings and beginnings
you have directed and handled so well.

Skin Hunger

Whether we are the person whose spirit has passed on or the survivor of one whose spirit has, the beginning challenge is "sensory hunger." We feel this initially no matter which side of life's veil we are on. Living together on earth, we enjoyed five great senses to interact: smell, taste, touch, see, and hear. Of these, we attach to each other emotionally in the greatest degree by use of the last three. When these familiar interpreters between lives have become altered, there is an initial period of alarm. This loss of physical familiarity is also called "skin hunger." For the Sweet Ones this realization of lost contact occurs when they call out from the Other Side to loved ones to see and touch the endless grandeur before their new eyes (the stage of Surprise). For us it obviously begins the moment a loved one's body is removed for burial.

After a shared material lifetime with each other

here relying on the physical senses, death appears to have severed all possible sensations. Those of us yet human may even find ourselves clinging to sensory leftovers such as clothing, colognes, voice recordings, and other things. These leftover snippets are, of course, soothing; but insofar as separation anxiety, they are not much more than a stopgap. The truly enduring way to remain in touch with loved ones after a death is to develop your unseen sensory antenna, which is now the main language of the Sweet Ones. This is, of course, your Sixth Sense. There will be new signs and symbols to create and to recognize. You will rely more and more upon your expectation and imagination. It will take some training, and as you try, you may sometimes miss the mark—just like any other language study. But as long as you realize that, as a spiritual being, your sixth sensory ability is always within you; all you have to do is trust in its presence, dust off the tools, and practice. There are many teachers just like me who are willing to get you started.

Fear of Abandonment

Each of us has a natural fear of abandonment. This arises from our ongoing clouded memory of spiritual Origin. We cannot remember leaving our Source, so we carry with us on earth a subtle sense of being abandoned or, worse, banished by God. For as long as we fail to recall our divinity, many moments in our material lives will stir up a fear of such rejection; and, the desperation to regain something lost will silently ride along. Moments of death are at the top of the triggers. We feel left behind if someone else dies, and we fear being forgotten if we are the one nearing death. There are, of course, many other sparks to this abandonment fear, but each time we rev it up, precious energy is lost in false anxiety rather than living out loud in Love. Watch for any thoughts of fear which arise; particularly the scare death raises. Ask your angels to help you transmute them to beauty and calm. Develop the knowingness that you are traveling here by your own free will, means, and timing. Each of us may not forever walk in step physically with each other, but abandonment across our birthright is a fallacy. When your thoughts wander to this fear, particularly when death arrives, breathe into it and say, "Be gone fear; you have no power over me." Here is one of my favorite acronyms for you to write and reach for:

F.E.A.R. is: **F**alse **E**vidence **A**ppearing **R**eal.

Speaking of emotions, there is one more understanding to set right about our immersion into human sorrow; particularly a death. It is usually offered when we experience a death, that there is "no set amount of time for grieving." With love and respect for these personal wishes, they may not be the healthiest idea for preserving your fragile sense of authority when death occurs. Remember, it is the perceived *loss of control* that lengthens the sorrow. To rest upon the invitation to take all the time in the world for the most dreadful feelings may be just what maintains them. There is always a choice.

Emotions are all the possible feelings resting in the aura nearest the ethereal aura (white outline) which is the connector to our physical body. We absolutely own the contrasting emotions in this energy field, and we either intentionally or habitually attach them to our thoughts, words, and senses. We have, of course, attached to physical death the most miserable kind of feelings. They are by habit easily accessible at the first sign of such shock. No one is arguing it is your choice to take as much time as you wish to be with unexpected woefulness; rather, the challenge is for you to become your own time-keeper. Following is one way.

Begin the habit of naming your emotions as they arise. You might even develop your own "shortlist" of opposing feelings. As I always say, "You can't tame them if you can't name them." Even if an emotion seems to have taken you by surprise, give it a name and add it to your list. Next, stop and decide how long you wish to allow any named emotion to beat within you. Plan to set with a clock the amount of time for which you will endure each. Shorten or lengthen decided times for the emotions as you wish, each time you use this practice. The goal is to extend the amount of time in your life to emotions which raise you up.

One of my favorite material tools to advance this kind of emotional ownership is a standalone timer (a bargain at any dollar store). Crank the dial on the timer to whatever measure you wish. In this discussion we are dealing with depressing emotions. Be and feel the emotion for as long as the timer ticks. However, when the timer rings, purposefully change the sad feelings by entertaining those things to which you attach the opposite; that is, feelings of joy. You can program this by developing and keeping within reach mental or physical cues which raise you up to laughter and smiles; for instance, a funny picture or story, or a recording filled with people laughing. Sit with those feelings for a newly selected period of time; thereby giving yourself permission to enjoy. This small exercise will raise you above panic by reminding you of your authority. You're invited to do this because when we allow grieving to dominate our earthly procession, we are taking the easy-out from participating in our own divine purpose and transformation. Learn to separate healthy longing away from uncontrolled misery.

This is a wonderful place to share with you one more personal story.

> *When I was 3 years of age, along with my sister, who was almost 5, and our mother and father, I went to an outdoor picnic held by the church community. My sister and dad went off together to find a table for our fixings. There were lots and lots of people and lots of grassy areas. Mom was holding my small hand at her*

side. Grass was pretty much all I could see from my height, except for my mother's calves and the tip of her yellow pedal-pusher pants. I could, however, hear lots of laughing voices above my head, and more and more legs seemed to be arriving; they all had similar white shoes. Then the awful moment came to pass.

My mother let go of my hand – perhaps to hug and greet a few of her nearby friends. I was waiting alongside her, but I think my mother turned in a different direction – or maybe I did. Suddenly, when I next looked up for the familiar color of pedal pushers, they were gone. There were legs and those white shoes everywhere, but I could not see my mom's. This could only mean I had lost my mom or worse she forgot me and left without me! I immediately started crying out in panic over my abandonment. I can still hear that little voice in my head, "Mommy, Mommy, Mommy, MOM-EEE!"

Just before I ran myself out of breath, a miracle overtook that crummy fear. My mother squatted down to my level, and the beautiful face I knew was back before my eyes. My mother held me to her outstretched hands and kept saying over and again, "Honey, honey, why are you crying? I'm right here." Oh my gosh! All was well in my little world, and I knew my mother would never abandon me – not then and not ever.

Life After Life

What I have kept in my heart from my little girl story is that while there would be times when my mother seemed to be out of sight, she would never be out of reach. This is how my trust and belief in our connection evolved. By the age of five, when I could see my angels and began talking with them, they reassured me, this is exactly how it is life after life. I offer you this same genuine assurance when you respond to death's separation. Truly, even at the experience of death, none of us are without each other. We just are no longer living side-by-side in a material environment. You are a wholly spiritual being; simply make a decision to stretch!

As long as our material world thrives, every one of us, here on earth, will, by our own design, reach our own spiritual "Moving Day." We will dismiss our earthly odyssey and shed our bodily vessel. We may have fulfilled our earthly intentions, or perhaps not. Whatever ending we may have chosen, in our new beginning we will enjoy The 5 Stages of Afterlife, starting with Surprise.

We all know by now that letting go of pointless attachments to other persons, as well as addictive habits acquired, is great for our physical well-being. The most obvious of these are attachments to those we hold in anger, hurt, or disdain; and habits formed from anxiety and lack of confidence. Keeping in mind, there are five Stages of Afterlife and one is "Concern," think about the following.

It is healthy for our immortal Spirit's wellness to practice detachment now. If we divorce some of our needy or limiting attachment issues while in the body, we are less likely to linger in the afterlife stage of Concern or backward pull. This means we will more readily advance our returning Spirit's progress through Attunement and Acceptance. And that means the stage of Bliss will so much sooner move us away from the material weightiness we once thought was a great idea. The process of afterlife travel is evident, but we may do a little spiritual pre-planning here on earth rather than "hide and wait."

Finally, try to remember we do continue to play a role in our loved one's development on the Other Side. This offers us choices and even sacrifices to consider for their behalf. It not only means releasing our clinging tragic emotions but also cleaning up our own foolish behaviors – either of which naturally pull deceased loved ones earthbound in *concern.* Share instead your laughter, dreams, and celebrations when connecting. Give your best to your life so they may freely thrive in theirs.

No matter how well you finally do here on earth, one thing is easily for certain. When you die, you will be greeted and entertained by minions of spiritual friends, some more familiar than others – including those you once loved on earth. This likely raises the question, "Will they know me?"

First of all, as explained early on, there is a group of spiritual angels who assign themselves to individuals as personal guardians. We each have two to three such angels at our physical side throughout our lives. These angel guardians remain solely our angels from birth through death and thereafter. Think of these angels as your BFF's from heaven. They are joined with you, love you beyond any human failing, and offer assistance to you whenever you ask. For sure, they do and will continue to know you very well.

Secondly, all spiritual beings (which means you as well) who have spent time in the material body will carry over remaining, predominant personality traits to the afterlife. Think of our time on earth as a physical event, *filled with physical events*. We are the all-terrain vehicles and acquire the journey's particles. Just as a sandy earth residue remains after a good earthly hike, our human personality permeates the new spiritual form after death for some time. We will recognize these vibrational signals in each other with super-consciousness. Additionally, our energetic auras, including the emotional aura, will remain intact. So yes, when you cross over, you will be well-known. You will also have a choice in selecting reunions.

You're invited to change the way you see our worlds. *All* physical beings will return to spiritual Origin. Source will manage the "merging of lanes." Remember, you will have a choice of encounter. Just remain confident in knowing all that comes from God is 100% Love, Light, and Intelligence. When any one of us sheds the body and material world to return Home, this same Love, Light and Intelligence will cleanse any dark energy or seemingly unredeemable human life. This is the part of the resurrection process I call **G.G.T.C**:

God's **G**ot **T**hat **C**overed.

In all the wisdom the angels have passed along to me, outstanding is the truth, death is a part of our *whole* life, wherein everything is created in Divine and Perfect Order, without end.

Remember the Five Stages of Afterlife the angels have shared which I have passed on to you. Write them upon your heart: ***Surprise, Concern, Attunement, Acceptance, Bliss.*** Repeat them when others you cherish leave before you. Rely upon their beauty when your turn with death approaches. Do not fear. Do not cry. All the heavenly hosts will be near telling you, just like my mother once said, "I'm right here."

I hope the pages of this book bring you a little greater understanding of death and dying, the spirit world, and your own amazing Journey Back Home. I hope you have greater trust in the true proximity of those loved ones you perceived unreachable after material death. And I hope you now believe connecting with them is always within your power.

It is true there will be twilights, and there will be dawns. There will be many on earth until there are few, and each parting will bring its sorrow. Trust the reunions you seek will one day become apparent. In the meantime, when you fear drifting apart, soothe your grieving heart with gratitude of all before your eyes and animate it in your life. Look, don't wait for your charm and blessings; welcome them, don't shy away, and let it be known you're asking for more. All the beauty and grace you ever need to master this material life is intrinsic to your True Spirit. You are a divine artist on earth, and it is time to express your beautiful purpose. Your free will is your palette of choice, and you are the producer of the magnificence of our Source, which is 100% Love. This is what we came here to do. All the angels assure me, it will be much easier if we keep in mind, we are first and foremost spiritual beings. As such, we are a Trace of Heaven.

So then, until we meet again – wherever that may be – here is my True Spirit's heart for all your tomorrows:

> *I see You. I honor that place in You in which the entire universe dwells . . . I honor the place in You which is of love, of truth, of light, and of peace . . . and I know that when You are in that place in you, and I am in that place in me, We are One.*

About the Author

Nancine Meyer is one of the most highly recognized, gifted spiritual teachers and intuitive guides of our time. She is an extremely skilled, authentic, sixth sensory professional and expert Angel communicator of many audiences and many years. She is an advanced Law of Attraction coach; successfully helping thousands to manifest prosperity. To reach this result, Nancine combines her Angel-guided revelations and six sensory skills with her practical comprehension of human resources learned from her many years in corporate business.

Nancine is beyond a doubt a very talented author and informed writer who has previously brought to us *The Lighter Side of Prayer* and many other periodical works. A well-known motivational speaker, Nancine brings her enthusiasm for each person's success into plain light in a truly personable, straightforward, and entertaining style. While all of Nancine's work is very loving, encouraging, and results-focused, *Traces of Heaven* is perhaps her most healing work to date.

Nancine has an extensive, intuitive coaching practice based in Surprise, Arizona. Seeing the Angels as they live and work among us in the material world, she named it *Main Street Angel* more than fifteen years ago. Today, many of Nancine's followers believe she is, herself, the "Main Street Angel." She is a genuine, caring, lightworker who is remarkably qualified to provide Angel readings and success coaching by distance, as well as in person.

To schedule an event or inquire about individual sessions, please visit:

https://www.MainStreetAngel.com

email her at Nancine@MainStreetAngel.com

or phone (623) 544-3304

Gratitudes

I love writing gratitude! Expressing gratitude is often preceded by the exclamation: "Wow!" That being so, to all of you who trust in my intuitive clarity, welcome my teachings, and cheer me on to do more, I invite you to close your eyes and imagine a huge high-five as I exclaim, "WOW!" You are holding another result of your love and confidence in hand; this book, *Traces of Heaven*.

My appreciation as the author begins with a "hooray for you" to the angels and spirit guides who are always with me and respond quickly to my writing hang-ups along the wording process. When each structural solution became clear, I could hear them say, "We told you it would be okay." When I oftentimes grumbled, they always appeared to be smiling and making that "eye roll" motion, followed by celestial giggles. I know the angels are listening in right now, so I will say, "For sharing your supernatural wisdom, your great love, and outstanding patience, Thank you, Angels!"

Getting back to our world, I'd like to point out that although the angels give resolve, there could be no book ending without its beginning. I could not bring these pages to your eyes without its initial incentive to provide answers to your hearts' delicate questions. I am very grateful for each of you here on earth who persist in seeking your true spiritual identity and share your experiences and curiosity with me. Thank you for your desire to remember, and for trusting in my sixth sensory ability to advance your journey.

If you know me, you are aware that I love to greet and speak. Among my blessings are caring audiences and devoted clients who afford me the opportunity to share my divine message and remind them of their own true Light. I wish I could mention all of these cherished individuals, but there are truly too many occasions, and too many names, to include on so few pages. If you are reading this and do not see your name in print, I will never forget you. Simply open your heart chakra and feel the energy of love and gratitude I am sending to you, right now and always.

I am very fortunate to enjoy special friendships throughout my life's story, both new and long-standing. In particular, I appreciate these generous people who are always ready to love, share, and recreate with me through all my ups and downs. Thank you for voicing your suggestions and affecting me with your laughter and joy: Susan Asbury, Craig Asbury, Nancy Krastine, Kristin Scott, Lynnae Jenkins, Shannon Switzer, Jo Ann Krones, Larry Krones, Sandy Belmonte, Dan Belmonte, Tina Ferguson, Caren Haeger, Sharon Thielenhouse, Jan Bailey, Cathy Brenner, Michelle Coates, Debbie Manning, Pat Wright, Judi Leazzo, Caren Cantrell, Mary Gutierrez, Toni Meier, Deb Graszer, Mary Lou Chapman, Madonna Maze, Peg Kusner, Sandra Forsey, and Sheila Leedy.

A few of these named friends merit an additional shout-out. Big hugs and thank you ever again to Shannon Switzer, Nancy Krastine, Kristin Scott, Lynnae Jenkins, and Susan Asbury. You returned my writer's enthusiasm to the project so many times when I was thinking of quitting. You are those darlings who subtly (so you thought) moved me forward by tossing into random conversation, *"So, how's the book coming?"* I hope you know I knew it! Thank you for each time you raised my writing spirits and thereby brought *Traces of Heaven* to fruition. You remind me of the angels!

I also wish to repeat gratitude to others of my friends who became so because of an original business relationship with me and my company, *Main Street Angel*. You people are amazing and truly make me look good. Thank you for getting to know me so well, and for "keeping me on." Sandy Belmonte and Dan Belmonte (Belmonte Printing), Deb Manning (Deb Manning Design), and Caren Cantrell (102nd Place, LLC).

Certainly, I have saved the obvious for last. I am so blessed to enjoy a loving family – husband, sister, nephews, nieces, cousins too! Thank you to each one of you for offering interest, love, and support for the healing work I do and the pages I write. I appreciate all the times you welcome me into your hearts and entertain my life with yours. In particular, my gratitude and special sentiment go to my generous, caring sister, Pat Nelson. Thank you for your constant interest in my unusual work, and for seeing me through the eyes of love no matter what I do. Our bond grows lovelier, and our laughter louder, year by year.

Finally, I give my crowning thanks to Gary Lees, who is an awesome musician, brilliant problem-solver, and passionate, devoted spouse. I am so grateful for your unconditional love and belief in me no matter what may happen. I know being around the "writer's cave" was not always easy, and I appreciate your understanding and support of me and my work. I am blessed to have you as my lover, my hero, and my best friend every day of our lives.

To all of you here, just imagine a standing ovation of praise. My angels have taught me to exclaim in triplicate, and so with all my heart, I say, "Thank you! Thank you! Thank you!"

Remember, I love You!
Nancine

www.ingramcontent.com/pod-product-compliance
Lightning Source LLC
LaVergne TN
LVHW020934090426
835512LV00020B/3347